ONLY WONDER

Poems

by

John M. Yozzo

ISBN: 978-1-936923-19-9

Second Edition November 2019

Cover Art & Design by Devey Napier

Village Books Press Cheyenne, Oklahoma

ACKNOWLEDGEMENTS

to Dorothy Alexander for the kind opportunity of this book.

to Devey Napier for the inimitable cover art.

to Terri Cummings for the exceptional editing; all errors and idiosyncrasies are my own.

to Jerry Bradley, Nathan Brown, and Roy Giles for publishing previous poems.

to Rayshell Clapper and Jessica Isaacs for their intellectual support and abiding love.

to Deborah Bailey for her insights and faith.

For Rita

who catalyzes me

CONTENTS

NUPTIALS

when I am gone
what will you keep of me?
do you know why
I ask rather than say?
who can know better than thee
(who loves Shakespeare)
how you love me
how you summon
me who muses you
me who ascends on your joy?

so – it progresses – a bottle for the newlyweds
but not so much the vintage we share;
let them grow to find distinct truths
amid confusions, strength amid complexities.
they marry near solstice, so let us
let them celebrate rebirth, the throbbing
rise of the year-god.

I throb yet, maybe daily, early rising
dawn-raiding as my love described
and am also replete to lie beside you
to mimic your slumber to swim
in your nocturnal rhythms because
I love marvel amaze at you
as my words flock to sunrise.

when I am gone, please keep
diurnal vigils to slumbers (yours)
and coffee (mine) and the peace
of this house we build daily in honor
of reminiscence and other complications
of our spirited cosmic inevitable love.

R & B

her floating breasts, soapy and slick
a nereid splashes in her bathing tub
and sings within her bonds, not the sea's;
oh that I could have forever her
to learn the fabric of her febrile form
and know the days' discovery of years in her
beneath her buoyant gaze
and fondly fret these gravities of love

AFTER ST. LUKE'S

man dies, we are told
and he is not happy, but these
subjunctions needn't constrict us.
a contrariety to fact, light
stays its oppositions
usurps a moment to forget
more prevalent subfusc deities
loneliness, night
jealousy and fear
a storm's luminescence or the
specific scene of a caress
are mere metaphors
for the moment the lone wolf
enacting primal ritual
lay circling down to sleep

KISS

softly like clouds
rolling purposeful
like mouths, slow
collisions of dough
kneaded wrestlings
suck upswooping
crash, a flicking
and thunder, rain
possible in the morning

EYES DILATED AT THE OPTHAMOLOGIST'S

if a poem is sense
as someone tried to convince me once
I can't read poetry for this poem:
A chatty irrelevant woman in the room adjoining
opining about death, as if she knows yet;
a country song whining indecipherable down the hall;
the sticking click of this burlwood clock
are all poem, and sighted, voiced, clean-smelling
and pure; unlike death she claims to understand
unlike the tree which died for burl and lost love
indistinguishable like life just down the hall

ASSENT

well, who said
anything would be fun.
easy maybe but satisfying
fulfilling? sorry
life was not meant
to be painless
nor the problems
of death solvable
life, some russian
said, was accepting
the loss of one joy
after another
so love (oh, for
example) is no
archetypical picnic
either; disease
informs the whole
the whole shades
the parts
why do we so love
for the moment
justifying a month
or a year? for peace
bridging horror, an
arrangement damning
chaos
Yup

CLOSED ON SUNDAY –
GO TO CHURCH

15

The road-sign Diner teaches
piety, lays to rest
one slumbering lust, but O
to have you for a quarter-hour
plumb those luscious darkling
taunts of pleasure, you
to bind and tickle
with innuendo

HOLY MOTHER

when I recall the musical taste of my pubescent youth –
Paul Revere and his raiders, Dave Clark's 5, the early
    Stones –
I embarrass myself; who was what little goofball trying
the Raider shuffle (embarrass myself) who was I –
God's little acolyte to the Roman mysteries, who
    cheated
Good Friday's vow of silence with surreptitious
earphones on the early Beatles?
day one in purgatory;
I was uber-catholic, confirmed at 9
called by the Bishop to recite my Pater Noster;
would read the ironic Lives of the Martyrs
as Saturday game prep for football;
the second-best altar boy St. Mary's ever made
who served a Sunday High Mass unassisted to earn
a special blessing from our grave pastor.
was bestowed Outstanding Eighth Grade Boy
photographed alongside a girl four inches taller
and my true first love my first eight years; was deemed
"too serious" on parent-teacher night
by a nun who never smiled…a humiliating epiphany
as naively I waited on that morsel of praise.
& within a month, I was smoking Parliaments
I stole from my parents' stash, sneaking Falstaffs
in the glass kegs and punching every son of a bitch
who sneering rhymed my last name with that clown
and five months on tasted my first Pauline carnality
on the lightly mustached lip of a randy 7th grader named
    Angela.

I stayed with Mother Church another dozen years
through the exiles of good if ambivalent young priests
through the shepherding of lonely hard-drinking
    pastors
through the sad indictment of a non-catholic wife's
    erosion
of my faith… have struggled twice to kick "lapsed" cold
    turkey
only to fail and have left a church for long as ever I was
    in one;
bound now for hell and dying to believe.

CORRELATIVES

she is rain all touching
feeding gentle, she makes thankful
for the wet contrast, stirs
cloud and air and memory;
fitting are her rare storms
tumbling noisily on window and sky
murmuring off
reclaiming like thunder
inclusion like rain
encompassing: ubiquitous
and welcome for the fall

DREAM

you, prepared to leave
stacked bags on the porch
the pooch, confused
bee-lined you to me
shooed and back;
I, determined, had but two
chores to complete soon
to help you with your task;
I, distracted, meandered
back to you, the recycling
set out and you had gone

POWER OUTAGE

after love, the words failed
you rescued me from a year
there was not a thing to say
neither thank you nor please
love only me, as you were
then loving me I was then
loving you when words went away
when tomorrow's afternoon shied
away from memories
and need for dreams

CHEAP PIPERS

these we pursue
for the seeming searing
magic of their breath
the singeing snarl
of words past love
make us beasts
to be off-loaded
dancing to our demise

SINGLE GRIZZLY BEAR

Charmingly deluded curmudgeon
Seeks cute-as-a-bug's ear
Philosophically-inclined
She-bear for scruffs
& scritches
& huckleberry pie

KAREN

grant a phoneme left or right
make language work its sway
I'll drive til night makes way
for light and wander
quiet streets and alleys, but
were I to alight at your driveway's door
would a morning beer I pray to greet
or wonder, light of waning, or dark
a longer ride to bed

MUCH ADO

she seeks recovery from an addiction
which too long eluded her;
she was doubly taken
and doubly doomed by it
and her unwilling obsession;
he has found solace from his pain
in a new solipsism, the narcissism he
was told and so long believed was
wrong; running daily miles and
sculpting his new self suffice
for now, and he's yet young enough
to make his own differences;
another dead love seeks the way
of Tao and young, too, finds comfort in ideas
filling one appetite with food for another;
his needs too will fail fulfillment
but we savor our moments and search
among our images for the clean shrill
incontrovertible whatever;
all she knows is loss and savors what
she can manage, plans never to lose
again, never to gain the hope that lies;
her salvation is her loss, waiting clenched
against the next storm, she hopes for better lies

DOUBTS

can it possibly be as good
the other side of dawn;
will sampling beyond our means
as we do all the time now
seem so sinful and real;
will the vitality of spring
provide lilac splendors
elsewhere, or if today's
virtues are the sweetest
we'll ever know, will they
show us only then
those other sides of now

ASCENSION

stripped of significance
she was girl and primal
home before dark fires
pure before the savagery of need;
stripped of world
she made dignity
the upright disposition
of breasts, the tawny
muscling of a matter, this
spring before the storm's dark breaking

SIC GLORIA

it never lasts, thank God
the terrible moment
and the breathless tumble
into what we know
death will be;
the patterns of her
mood, the changing face
the settling gaze
she is what she knows
and does what he cannot
express; her kind nestled
in his observation
will never fail

JOJO

I wonder what she saw in the mirror
that instant before the trigger;
was it the painful weariness
she showed us a quarter hour before
or resolution, her sad sweet knowledge
of the painful end of life she foreshortened
as if to counter the inexorable loss
of sanity in some thumbing at fate
and found instead a longer sleep
than the rest she told us she so badly needed

PASSAGE

as time goes
this anniversary puzzles
a memory barely loosed
withstands embellishment;
the sweetest soft somnolence
of latter couplings belies
the tender tossings
of our fevered summer's first;
ours is not a vague chronology
of the world's hard urgings or of
our own singular divergence after love
but tempers mad fondlings
gives more of peace than missing you
retrieves, and remembering you dares hope for

AUBADE

you will know this is for you
by firelight late abed
when an ember glows as if
in dreaming you'll arise
to tread known hallways
to find I am but a ghost
a memory like a poem.
you will know this is for you
by lamplight aglow in mornings dark
as the house awakens from its winter
cold to warmth, the thrill of coffee and of love;
you will know I am near in darkness
the rush of sleep upon you
the jostling play of wakefulness
the cold snap of morning the
slumber of a careless afternoon;
you will know I am yours in words
and miles time cannot abridge;
I am yours for distance, a paradox of life;
another? to sleep to awaken
to die so we might only live in peace

REMINISCENCE

I am sorry, but raised on guilt
I see your need for now, the commission
of soul for yet another past-due
account; your asking
indicts me to remind
how far I have slipped
to overlook your need
and this vale tears me
to pieces. bless me.
whatever absolution results
I am my sin

EDENIC

in the pool opaque by last light
a water-nymph plashes in her fundament
her lyric, like flowers, dancing on the waves
her countenance in-turned
bespeaks the magic of her world
ancient, destined and serene
this smile of gold
in an age of bronze, brazen like war
she is peace, apace from gold to Gold

IN RETROSPECT

after all is said
I love you
after all
after life, after love
all fear and fears of loneliness
after all is done
I am, I love
after

VALENTINE'S OR LOVE

you are the closest to right
I got in years, the prize
I do not need to reach for
a trophy I will not inscribe.
I, too, know about prizes;
I yearn and have been the yearning
but you will know this is yours
like a raven strand on a wheaten pillow
like one blinding sunray piercing clouds
and years of storm

HERSELF

amazed herself all
fluttered coyly flirting
with her self-sexual not mast-ur-ba-tory
soft as a kiss she kisses herself
her hand, an idea and likes her flavors
with lots of in-ter-stic-ing of comma—
suggesting
the
wait
is
worth
the
wait
it will be so
Good without punctuation
without these endless
endings, these
stops and goes
almost
something
amazing

DEATH AND TRANSFIGURATION

we wonder at the stasis
its serenity devolved from what toil
satiety gained at what cost
its nobility, its bearing, the
security in-turned of the gaze;

the fall is less worthy of note
our feet are sliding all the time
we trip all over, scab over
suffer the intrusions of life
into our lives but this too
is only quibble; the death
is the moment of proof--how one
dies belies a life sometimes--as even
Eurystheus goes down nobly for a change;

some recoil is possible, recovery not inevitable
is properly anticipated; we learn, adaptive
as we are, to lose and to climb
our tears yet staining our trust;

then we meet up again at stasis
wonder how a line does not bend
marvel at what serene closed secrets
the mask enfolds, what knowledge the lips
close upon, into what hearts her enigmatic eyes
like necessity, like an otherworldly god
gaze cursing

LIFE DEATH TIME LOVE SCENERY

any surprise the themes recur?
only this blustery late spring day
does death seem far, the sun
strong in the midday sky
water a metaphor for everything
fluidity, lightness evaporates
before we know them;
a dog dies in a novel and we cry
art is biographical, too close
we see our own pups dying
but love is individual;
no one knows our sorrows
or relief when she capitulates
and love is happy endings;
the sea is companionable
free-flowing with associations
with those we beg to trust
else life at the beach is only
meaningful in a mind unfocused;
pain, personal, always focused
focuses wisdom
our gaining knowledge only exercise
hit or miss, the shot in the dark
a toss in the skins of the living

OFFICE HOUR

you are waltzing through my time
like a stranger passing the window;
at first I frame and isolate you
pane by pane by partial view
and though I find you remarkably
lovely, this limited perspective
is all I can afford; you are a
singular exacting replica
of carefully constructed dreams
and my temporary sorrow is to linger
in this unfulfilling gaze; I cannot reach
you as no door permits my passage
into your world there, this wall holds
fast and this silly fascination merely
tickles. the time it takes
you to scamper across this stage
is the inkling I will ever know you

SCRIBE

the girl and the book so limned
set upon this threshold, this moment
the semblance of God without his power
lies in the empty page; she fills pages
with memories, harsh at times; they lie
committed and at times best closed upon.
a goddess to her task daily
she ordains a day's events with tools
like her sacred woodworker's—she planes
life to mold its frame, rights the angles
verso, recto, and plumbs mightier depths
than carpentry admits.
still bound, deskbound, she curves
her text, preferring to the machinations of words
processed, gaining her voice by hand, like a clerk
making her code indispensable in script secreted
yet necessary to its purpose, scrutable only to
the encoded and initiate.
this is the world she inscribes daily
each voice each memory a moment
in the streams of life she shallows daily
to savor this peace, her resting place

GIFTWRAP, OF SORTS

life is a blob of glass
a disc of world floating an ocean
a blear of conscience like a dream
but spins madding beyond sense
an unplanned goulash of flavor
a secret smudge of a lover's lip on crystal
a smear of dust deftly a keen brush
of thumb passing removes.
life is love lapping moistly at spectacles
giggling games of puppies unwilling
a kitten with bed fur in complete repose
the drear and the mundane of lives
troubled—worse, dulled—is life too
the blank of fear, the clutch at heart of loss
the ghostly wisp, a blob, a blot
the bleeding of energies saved or refulgent.
life is at times merely the mud of words
smartly seasoned, a slumgullion
with every so fortunate
and a little adventure in it

MAZAMA

the passage of time sits me humbly down
to recall this night years ago, you
fully naked, sheeted sleeping trustful,
so perfectly our first month went
we were impetuous and young
in a Victorian betrothal
you, sleeping, a child with finger to her lips
made calm the night and perfect our musted
grownup urgings. me, now as then, easily
distracted by your slumbering form, yes,
breasts, and the iridescent innocence
of your face; which saved me then
from pitiless confusions, which
now endears me when
the years' passage
saddens but redeems

COCKTAILS

let's say we
were fortunate to
know *presque vu*
to learn that we
would die in love
and know despite
our sorrows it
will all end happy
and correct so
that tonight we
could get drunk
and cuss the fragments
of our dark

DAUGHTER

do not blame her
she performs but
what she's made on
her grip of life
defined by knowing
loss acutely, her joy
a *jete*, falling from peak
to a respectable recovery
her grasp of things
joyfully tenuous, clutching
mystery, serenity and life
in ways unlike those hoarding
too frightened to conceive
what lies beyond
the bathroom door
after the shot

REMAINS OF THIS DAY

perhaps, once again, I will discover
sweet mystery, the accident of grace
first loss, the gold which cannot
stay our fears of the dark, which
will not illuminate the mysteries
of faith. we will sip sustenance
undeserved, and give sustenance
unpresumed: what to lose?
what to gain? the pendulous
motion of equipoise makes metaphor –
sex, like celebration
felicity, like wisdom
festivity, in place of love

PUT OUT THE DOG

everyone even woman
sips the precious flower
plucks the stem
to suck the blood;
everyone eats precious
food, devours, defiles
defends, everyone even
wife

THEY KNOW NOT

she sat in her motorized
chair waiting on the elevator
hunched against a world
afraid of freaks she
awaited instead the
buttons' illumination.
she sat across my lap
half-dressed and cried
goodbye to a special friend
time in which to feel
young, in which to try
heart against mind

SAY GOODBYE

a memory like a poem
you destroyed to forestall
questions about who I was
to you, photos put back baubles
donated to others less bewildered
less tangled, less troubled by loves
in their past tenses, safer
to live in future imperfect;
perfecting the present, I am
not even remembered, not like
death, **memento mori**
or rest, **requiescat in pace**
or a hand cupping you like love
through the storms of our sad dreams

SPRING

in the far corner of the fridge
stays a remnant of her love
unseen, a pitcher of tea, molding
pods on its bottom side. I grieved
not for her love, which uncatholic
considers such a thing not untidy
but draw comfort in young
rabbits joyfully in the yard
gamboling mindless of rituals
off in kitchens, unobsessed

IN KIND

our beauty was the dark
specific felonies performed
in silence; we talked for years
wondering if to… were we the casual
Freudian hungers for what—esteem?
the Daisy Miller defense, or darker
passions, as dead poets warn?
we ate our desires and grew into need
your dreamless eyes, their depths
of what reals us, your tensile grip of me
the flame of your strength
you fucked me, uncoiled me, me you loved
in our dark, our sweetest
sweetest loveliest crime

SOLSTICE

in the sunroom sea-green by last light
she sets candles curling
upward, the fan spirals
softly squelching fears of their demise.
he assures her back to vertical
his horizontal her intent
amid soft squashings and murmured
couplings all aglow he wonders
at peace in moments inexorably.
she dabbles to teach her discipline
borne of love and candles

LONG DISTANCE

so practical as
I detail my Thursday's
goals of exercise, she yawning
reminds me it's twenty til Friday
languidly between sighs
her voice peeks out of slumbers
waiting for the end of my
nocturnal musings on her thighs
the mood of her week, menstruals
and a little tummy-bloating.
pills she'll buy with the money
more easily sent than love, more
useful than this fondling urge
to know her past midnight
I am tomorrow and one-hundred sit-ups
forever behind

PASSOVER

in these crystal hours
of vision, where the
moment in arms
is the magic those
sun-blasted days
can provide, we
pray for omens
to spirit horror
from monstrous pangs
of love.
beneath this vernal
seaside moon, we relent
to clarify our need
face down our nightmares
and pray belatedly
to be spared

DENVER

the metallic morning's gray
needed that cigarette's pluming warmth
the living death in your painted eyes
foretold the need in your request
and painted a like hunger
in my unknowing mouth;
how easily from this past
I'd have played creator to your void
only shaken, sidestepped the morning's
dim refuse and thanklessly glided
by another bleeding Christ

APOLLO

your unmade bed held no secrets
for the curiosity of my lusts
the rhetoric of thank you, no, poured
drinks, made tour of the house
saw patterns in unions repast
myth has no answer for that moment
missed, the arrow arching ever downward
brings death from the warrior unseen
uncelebrant the ring forbids
its circle charitably small

BETTY

I don't feel 8:23 a.m.
four cups down, the grounds
soaking the morning's classifieds
mushrooms chopped wanting
wrapped, returned to their keeper
burger set by, relegated fallback
if chicken rotated to dinner status
can't go the distance
do I shave my legs or run
a dishwasher three-quarter full first
I don't feel supportive
of his needs today, was stoical
though tense, distracted in rebuff
last midnight, but will rally
a card or single rose on the lapis
tray, must wax, at least Endust
the table
don't feel my age (but whose?
not the perky oblivious I was once
'don't know what you've got til it's'
shot to hell
we try and err
grow old and die, yet inwardly
young; better the loveliest of cherries
than the dogwood blooms frozen
black by the late spring snow

VENUS HAS HIPS

Venus has grippable
hips and squeezable
parts and lovable
Stuff (one does not say
cunt & clit & nipples in lipping
the virtues of a goddess)
she has a dark side
musty warm and overflowing
whiffs of magnolia and oak
and fucks outdoors where
she can make her room
Venus is golden and wheat
and ivory-feathered and green
blue hazel cocoa-eyed as she
pleases and she pleases and
bites and pulls at hair
tuggly and fills with such
abundance as she empties
each stalk of manly life
and drives away
in her red sports
convertible

NO ARCHETYPICAL PICNIC

the sullen stinging blasts
of November reanimate ancient
agonies and carnalize the saddest
stories ever told; she walks away
into, he assumes, the months'
forthcoming, and the forgettings needed
for healing, and the returnings home;
he re-enacts all the old goodbyes.
she sees love, he descends
into brooding over means
she knows the rush into arms
and tumbling ascensions;
in their first kiss, he sees her
dressing once more for home
he knows, in the dilemma of this love
their dilated breathless musted rage
of love, they make food of each other
she ponders how to immortalize
a single moment; he knows solution
to her problem even as it takes her away
inevitable as decline, his fears
define his love of her

VIGIL

when he drinks to her
starts the old mellerdrama
all over again--half-dreaming
of lemonade, cherry peppers
her honey-blonde breasts
and sunflowers brings him
sharply up short, grimacing
at the glowing pain of ribs
not rightly healed after she
made of him a fleeing hood
ornament once
his pain does not engage
his heart, but rests in southern
hemispheres; hers inverted
a child they could not keep
stares pitilessly from out
their fractured pasts
so drinking bourbon from
a Farrah Fawcett insulated
mug is neither original but not
his problem now: he so longed
they prove exceptional but
love done 'em in

AT THE AIRPORT

my need for symbols and affirmation
sustained me the moment of your leaving
I thought of cleansing distance
the hope for better tomorrows
and sunlit silhouettes bespeaking
True Love as love should be
the car I thought yours melting
into the tarmac distance was
like many others that day, but
the sentiment's sustaining faith
amused me with hope
for a time
for a place

TRIPTYCH

a brooch unclasped set
free this longing so like love
for peace borne of storm

neon and thunder
spelled the clarity of need
in forging twilight

shadows of her sleep
bewitch the days of dream to
know imperfectly

HAIKU

nearly to heaven
far-flung purities of snow
MountainTop my love

PHILOSOPHY 101

after the stroke and our buoyant moments of hope
engendered by our clutching denial of your failing
we abided cheerlessly afraid for each new sign
of a loosed capacity, a missed step
were encouraged by your hunger for food
as even for…what, life?
as age ate you down to bones
when the kidneys failed as your memory how
even to drink water failed, we too
knew the pain in the bones of your life
a week before your death, as I watched you
sleep fittingly I marveled at the immediacy of your moment's
joy
I prayed to believe the awful inexorable unmitigated
goddamned
agonies of the world daily do come to peace
the welcoming, restful, dreadful peace
and so you died

FOR MOM, WHO SAID SHE WAS TIRED OF LIVING ONCE

Mother, your flesh hungering
for quiet must wait yet
in your time will death come, humble
captain, patient guide to loosen
sense and loneliness
our Father, yet in slumber, sheds
the darkness, ruined the fabric
of impatience, desire, and pride
and will meet you in the day
past midnight, sift gently through
and teach the metaphors--sleep
and joy and light and peace

FOR MICHELE

I saved the corpse
of a squirrel from the
street and sporting aim
of wheels; the day
began this way
hours intervening
saw life in late
winter's brown and
moist greens; still
the day for you
ended at dawn
you enter another phase of time
to learn of maturation and its
pains; your rebirth
pays in fear and end of innocence
the ruling constellations overhead
overstate their horoscopic claims
I never learned the facts of myths
but know instead life's patterns:
a night's calm belies the chaos of a world
a fresh grave scars the garden hill
and a girl passes into womanhood

WHERE I WORK

this desk, this resting place
where logos oversees ethos, confers
disciplines. I stare down themes
the rare with wit and semblances
of some knowing god. this
window, this escape, the career
and cavil of crows in the yard
they do not caw for me, and I
sit here unwelcome to join them
here this desk, this scene of sadness
the wrestle with words to convey
away the horrid deaths, the ignorance
of numbers, my own unwitting solemnities
this cat, chocolate, screwing its
purred head resolutely into my left eye
my non-writing hand perfunctorily mauling
defending my thoughts losing to these chocolate
ripping images of this live thing, bubbling happy
as should all moments of life, as I write
in pace, I miss you

IN PACE

I marveled at the smallness of you the first day we met
more spider than kitten growling bigger while you gargled food
promised nothing but fight your sole resolve to claim
your rightful place, a lap, a leg, a meal
you grew regal into feline, mottled more than calico
with the most delicate of pastel merely
glimpsed upon a belly rarely offered
preferring your fighter's crouch your entire life
but you loved me by your eyes, precarious and caring
as you perched ghostly soft on my haunch or belly
I feel you still more for abiding than alighting
soundlessly airlessly you appeared for shared denim
or to console me through my fevered nights
so when I folded you small into your box
I knew I'd feel you all the nights of my life
in light descendings, amid the awful, real emblems
of your passing, your resolute gaze
and your serene sustaining love of me

SCISSORTAIL

you would write this for me
yet I doubt I can for you
poets reading here assure of their
belief in logos, meaning, essence
significance, and at the end of the lonely
dim tunnel, our beloved happy to carry us home
Yonder John, your eyes will explode in fire
your skin crackle like parchment
we will need to grind those fine big
bones of yours but when done you
will emerge dusty and clean
a few-pound box easy
to transport ready
to wear upward

PERNIE

You loved hot sunshine and escaped your trapezoidal shack at the slightest encouragement from above.
Crawling hands and knees along the curb, you clipped and tugged at random weeds, a true sun-worshipper. What kind of world did you know? Voiceless and deaf you didn't heed the city-world except to pluck its curbside weeds and to soak in city sunlight. Was it true for you, as one hears it is for others like you, that the death of one sense intensifies those surviving? And, as part of some eerie compensation, did your landscapes sing more sensuously the songs you never heard and could never sing?

But your Nature's god was a perverse lover. Everything he compromised, you tenderly restored. Jealous, he deprived you of laughter and song. Forestalled a life outside and locked you in a coldly-lit world. You answered his greed by devouring all the sunshine you could hold. Through it all, you loved him fiercely, feebly, willingly, loved him grudging but never forsaking him. You asked but light and warmth for your cold silent shadows. So that when he gave you up, he left you aglow. Smoldering, slightly suffocating, suffering the touch of your fatal new love, you embraced the board floor of your cottage and consummated your new union in commingled dust and ash.

TO A HOUSE

all those years while
the real life of our lives
took place elsewhere
this house suffered here
not so much abused
nor neglected, as saddening down
so like the woman who lived
badly here, unable to feed
the needs of this place
as roof and panes and walls
instead nourished decay

so on our first official day
as orphans, way middle-aged
we return here to a house as old
as the mother we laid down
an hour before, to see the plans
of a stranger's future for the house
of our departed, ever-present dreams

stripped to her bones, lost limbs
orange-striped to signal excision
she was clean and warm
in her purified emptiness
hinting at the dreams of her new
life as a house, not just now
ready to die into ruin

REQUIESCAT IN AMOR

The day Dr. Terry gave permission
my Mom greeted Dad after work with two highballs:
Roger, I have to have a hysterectomy.
But, Agnes, that means we can't have any more children.

Drink up, Father. It's time. I'd offer suggestions
for one or two you could send back. But as Mom
once whimsically observed, *Were we Protestant*
I'd have stopped at Paul and Phyllis.

As the fifth of seven, this gave me to wondering
where, in my immediate world, I'd have been born.
But instead I looked up "highball: a cocktail made
of whisky with soda, served in a tall glass over ice cubes." And
thanks to F. Scott for that, too.

I doubt Roger and Agnes ever afforded dear whisky.
But soda is lovely as it does not appeal to the
kiddie palate, and the deeply etched glasses
yet draw my fingers to trace their edges, still
as I ponder where I would be born if not here?
Else, where do rerouted Catholic babies eventuate?

But a toast to Mom and Dad:
>What should heaven be
>But good whisky
>Soda from a seltzer
>Highballs without hangovers
>And sex with the Woman of your lifetime
>Without rhythm, and the babies
>God originally meant to send
>To the Presbyterians next door?

GRAVESIDE

I shared a cup of coffee
with Mom and Dad this morning
in that funereal fashion of libation
a draught for each of the lovely brew

I imagined bitter, gravesite grounds
for the grieving, faithful, loyal son
and true; in fact, however, the morning
was heart-wrenchingly lovely cool
to autumn's cold, but blinding and yellow

and the coffee was strong, tasty, and true
so to pretend there was nothing but grief to learn
nothing but the numerous unsealed, secret regrets
of a wayward son to mourn, is untrue
another lie of poets

a year ago, coffee this good, this brave, this loyal
would daily resurrect you yet, Mom;
Dad, though you fled sooner, your lessons
of the old aluminum dripolator are fresh
as Folger's today; and at thirteen, I, your obliging son
too was daily thrall to mild uremic aromas, and
the eager slurping scalds of our shared morning Mass

so for these forty years, I ponder wholly
the consecration of humble elements, prepare
offertory, the oblate's duty to host and monstrance
wonder, too, at literal transubstantiations
of carnation and sanguinity, and coffee beans
paying their morning ablutions
to the same obscure and darkling
God about whom we can only wonder

FOR ARNOLD

I don't know when again
it will be time for flowers
summer persists and autumn
no more descends as leaves
grotesquely clutch and drop
when flowers? when to care
so dear, so costly, daily
reminds of the hardness
of death, the suitability of dark
images? when shall come flowers
again, when death commends who
is appropriate and who shall ripen
yet? a world away, there shall be
flowers, forged in sunlit configurations
a world away, to decorate
this frozen grave in January

DEATH BEFORE DISHONOR

You will never wear your honor out
as today you perished in the maddening rout
you will never lose the dignity of the warrior
bravely fighting against the horrible foe;
your intellect intact as a crossword complete
vainly all the same against the ravaging storm.

Neither will there be a bathrobe-sighting, or the threat
of a you-tube unmasking on your own front porch:
Did you see how fill-in-the-blank awful—old—decrepit—
stoopid
Dr. W looked! at the grocery, or the hardware, or
    minding
your own goddamn business mowing your own front
    yard.

Instead, we will remember you hale
witty, bow-tied dapper, charming and smart, save those
who tended the ravening disease, and our last glimpse
    of you
that virile photo from your last symposium, or at least
laid out in your finest Sunday-go-to meetin'
God tailored set of clothes

MERRYMEANT

a little horizontal
(as e.e. would say) action
on the front fur rug is tender
for the seen, forgiven
for the unseen (but
can we see in darkness anything
or do we dream our long-
held hearts' desirings
your touch is vision less deceptive
more secure than memory
and here I ask you, curtail
me from these darker heavens
suspend your ninety-five less
pounds from my neck
and anchor me to life
remind me I will die
and who may explain why
I will not wish to leave
when my leaving day arrives

AS NOT TO WAKE YOU

I muff the hinge
to its furtive squeak
wait the heavy moment
to prove silent, I scrape
worn feet across the tile
another door, another song unique
thus punctuated, slumber
holds the house
I mean not to rupture
your fervid dreams, distracting
from a pain pressing against
hunger and unquenching need
I pad the morning floor
cross-stepping out from noise
to turn this fugitive
and final latch

STREET MISTRESS

I miss her gripped pedals
and firm padded handlebars
the hum of rubber at 10-15-20 m-p-h
the frictive tug of asphalt discipline
the telling twang of hamstring
the silent push of wind
up-rushing to delicate
cramped crescendo—
dismounted
this day meekly
no tumbling bruise
into wet canals
no reattachment required
for this, my loving, my daily
my sweetest ride

OUT AND BACK

on to bike-miles and the aspiration
of youthful vigor in aging joints
juke joints hip parlors hip flexors
on flexed puffed blistered cramped
toe-tips I move toward you; after
riptide seaside eyes wide by storms
tossed, higgly-piggling pony-dancing
monkey-shining, disconnect me
send me back for seasoning
been and gone, have I you
in rain and gale and storm
and ebb in thunder and ensuing mists
been and gone and rise and fall, ingress
egress outbound seaside air-pillowed
sky-floating desert-dancing
out and gone, been and back

SUFFICIENTLY PRESENT

I lose a piece of her every day
to the madness of bustle
the furrow of dreams
rushing to the edges of schedule
and dead-falls into sleep;
memory erases her face
the anger of her tone
perceptions of betrayal
I lose pieces daily
slivers glass-dancing
of another sort
and other disintegrations
I ken in darkness the woof and warp
the yanging yin, the obverse angles
of parallelograms, co-incidence
of planetoid physics' lovely
nothing, we lose in a moment
bit by bit, matter of memory
bits of each other to accommodate
cosmos expands to panorama
yet daily, by my small parallax
I lose essential bits of you
entropic heat, piquant nibs
of your molten love and light
epiphanies I cannot presently appraise
but know I must keen to believe

LIFE IS SWEET OR SUNDAY 4 A.M.

amid bourbon hot chocolate and feline Sophie
I brood happily on the nature of my illicit thing
after the number of years and the prospect
of bed as reward for these diurnal musings;
my cul-de-sac decidedly conservative
is not churchy, so my absence in driveway
and in worship will hardly subvert
their views of a curious man who
flies his flag, upkeeps his lawn, and who
noises about his house pre-dawn
with a flashlight, so as not
to alarm the neighbors

VALENTINE

most days she is silent
as the tomb before Easter
and Jesus dancing
holds her tongue in silent council
close to the vest, muted, zipped
yet when she falls into words
with a perceptible **fump** as snow
sings flopping from the warming roof
her music bakes the room to melody
caramelized tones rising as bread
a dulcet glaze on the cake that is her joy

HOW IT HAPPENS

it's not that I cannot
recall your lipping breasts
the day before we became
the hungered us, sustaining
half a dozen years and a thousand miles
it's not I lost the night
your porch light burned
your phone rang empty
as the love in your womb
the only role you ever dreamed
auditioning died frustrate
it's not I wouldn't
sadly recognize what we
knew years ago tomorrow
if we managed a table
in the sunshine with hope
for wine and the flirtatious
disregard for life outside
late lunches, and the world
curled up at curbside
waiting yet aware

MEMORY OF A GIRL

I will always be that boy
who touched you on the beach
while no one watched, we
imagined we owned it all, empty
a storm to the south in Mexico
urged self-preserving hordes toward home
while I scratched your name
in sand-script with an inadequate
spar of driftwood
we picked and struggled out
the windswept, wave-washed jetty
poured a Coors toast to Neptune
for love and 70s teenaged lust
for the most beautiful girl
in the world who would not
go topless to the wash but who
wafts me seaside forty years on

SEEKING WISDOM

up before light to tame
the darkening beasts, and worse
wrestle waking doubts of growing
daily vain against the reals of age
the rising falling days, their unalloyed
indictments of waste
as sleep squandered in favor
of chasing shadows and indiscretions
and cringing cuckoldry, and worse
the fruitless, nightly castrating
of a eunuch long since cut
what fears be these
what deaths so drear
that sleep seems nearly not so frightful
hardly to inspire this wrath of words
what then of losing her to another
when easily summoned are her eyes
her soft, safe kindness
her soft, soft love
so whom to wrestle this pre-dawn gloom
another, receiving of her love, undiscerning
yet even blessed as I—who should blame?
or time, which steals sleep but lends this
night to thoughts: one-eleven, three-fifteen
four forty-three, mere numbers in a zone
in the dark; what doesn't maim
makes me wiser? what fitful frets inure?

and this dark waxes to twilight, in this gloom
a little hope yet; in her shadows, the fundaments
of fear of loss, despair and truth
only inevitable, this loss of sleep
as wisdom herself lays truth aside
and I in shadow will abide til God uncomplicates
to swing away these gates of purgatory

STEALING WATER

it begins with the harmless klept of a bottle
shared backwash, strange recycling
moves to a game of who steals whose
and who will holler first, babying for justice
the injustice is thirst unslaked
innumerable quests to what fonts
addicting plunges into unstaked pools
before Ponce or other conquistadores
lay prior claim to the miracle flush
of happy madness, to confounding joy
a thirst unquenched, unslaked
the greeding poet hyperbolizes
here a taste, tomorrow maybe even torrents
raging from heaven, but focuses on the unswum
river, the unfallen cascade, this abiding gulf
rather than to offer praise for today's
blessed draught, Who fills and flows within me

ON READING KIERKEGAARD'S
SILENCE

and who are you when you are quiet?
what force do you revere?
wherein lies the deference most due…
God, or Something in nature –
when one first feels the awe
the breath-taking instance of what
he falls, blessed and weakened
to wonder what befell
to find peaceable love, fleshed love
nothing fearful in the hungering splendor of awe
imagines God in the smallest details
and wrongly draws up articles of hope
there is no time for hope; no peace in words
reiterates need – for silence and keening
for holiness and the reverence of strength

PRAYER

Deliver her from the toil of days
the man-managed agonies of time
schedules and deadlines
Deliver her to know bountiful love
the innate wisdom of eyes & instincts
the atemporal love of time
Deliver her from late-night temperings
of sadness and care, the shitting
inconvenience of life daily
and love 'eternally' promised
Deliver her to knowledge
of real love, daily suffering
the requisite struggle amid
faith and dreams
belief and hope

MORNING'S CALISTHENICS

if love is grace, faith inspiring
rosy dawn after the night's storms
what antithesis?
I would gnaw off a limb
to reverse time
reclaim a roseate hour of you
yet when that hour expires
so begins our past, and in the manner
of standing at crossroads
I choose the rigor I welcome
and Hope, as my road
to hell is already paved on it

AUTUMN'S SONG

when I no longer have you here beside me
will we be happier in another time?
will we frolic in flowered fields
after the field hospital, phantom
pieces of our hearts removed
to move each other forward
launch our new offensives;
to happiness, or plural, whatever
we must have to horror away
the demons loving and loss
to magic ourselves, or each other
or oneself, or no one at all
into believing baptisms of renewed trust;
when I no longer have you here to dream on
will we be happier in the morning's gloam
will we step lightly into the waxing day
after the first blinding, phantom shadows
of our wrongs disproved, moving
forward to evitable conclusions
to shed our worn defenses
to clutch at this new chance

LEAVING HOME

my best rib, the most
magnificent thing any god
ever made of bone
delivers us to this spot
of cooling peace
beyond the flames of Paradise
you are my Eden
every tree, each fruit of sustenance
and peace; you are cool water
against my scorching fear
you are patience, coiled anticipate
against the instant of rage
I move with you
I gauge your eyes, I read
your silent words
God is coming and the angel after:
when you declare
we can no longer be here
I am ready with you

THE ANSWER

eludes all but a few
the rest of our lives
resemble shopping lists
for bleach and bologna
true meaning is effable and elusive
a morning's quick harvest
of the day lilies' husks
the twist of a screw
to tighten a screen, tasks
forgotten, quickly done
but The Answer, an old man
once told me, *not to be
deluded by dreams,* compels
our hunger for the thing
the touch, the image
of meaning, something like
a puppy's tracking yesterday's
yard-clippings across
clean wet linoleum

A VICTIM OF DIVORCE

your painted crags of mortar
know the loss of brick and stone
your textured ceiling panels
forget their sagging timbers' song
the cool damp vacuum of decay
belies your solid floors, thus
unjointed and dismembered
your cornerstone weeps
for nothing left to found

THY FOOT SHALL SLIDE

it is a kiss
it bites the upper lip
it offers beaver teeth
flirting fevered
it raises eyes and mouth
it plumps awaiting
it is perfect

SIMPLE BEAUTY

unshod
unwired unpainted prewashed
full and rounded
warm and promising
in black camisole
and baby night shorts

GRATITUDE

the mercy of loves, the tending of strength
and hands, the beautiful, personal gnarl of the grip
the hungry re-visitation of lips, tongues, tugs
we repeat, lather, rinse, we are iterations
of memories, we need – the desire for anchor
the assurance of this unique, exclusive blush
of the oxytocic hug…happy after? laughter
rises from the falling raptures, the filling hilarity
of your…*love?* when fuck is the fit-fullest
paradigm to unmask this aching lovely thing

SEA COW

my manatee, my bobbling
sea-bubble, my laughing cow, immersed
emerging from a wine-dark sea
no pirate Botticelli
unscurvied, unrummed, nor peg-legged
got Venus right, skating like a festive
luscious poem, she surfs shoreward
a'shell in retreat from Ouranos's
severed and quivering loins
but you my chuckling foam-bucket
besot me beckoning: to sea, to sea
come bob with me
I am your sirened slave, sotted, monocloptic, tattooed
galley-thrall, for whom your blubbing, wafting booty
your snorkeled barks are grandest art subtexted
bugging your hither-coming cow-orbs
bubbling subtle, just below wave-length

ANGEL OF THE LANDFILL

she was diaphanous with stilettos and fiercely cleavaged
the day she descended from the heavens to the landfill –
garbage apotheosized
the dump monkeys froze
in abject awe and reverence
perched apelike, awaiting
a bosomy glimpse of heaven
shy for monkeys, almost appalled
a goddess maybe, princess surely
she was be-gloved to her elbows
in cow skin, new and fragrant
(was it Io's or Europa's eucharistic offering?)
she set down one pointed lovely shoe
into the dump muck, but as cauterized
by too humble earthen clay, she recoiled
shrilling, like the freshly de-veined Father of her Sky
and lofted back into the truck
shivering afresh with dump cooties
the monkeys hummed and swam
toward the carriage but her four-wheeled
apple-red cart trudged her to safety
the lovely glove she shed in mire
of earthen glue reminds the chimp boys
of heaven, amid dreams one might find
the luscious limb to fit that sleeve

INTRICACY

your breath is fluid
proof of our desire
hankering for the six seconds
to learn your flavor
to take your hunger
I am caught in wonder
about your intent
is this our now, shall I
abide, or strike flowing
into memory long abed
are you what I think this is
determined to forge through
less perfect elements of time
this place, other loves
will you leap atop
as I play fundative
underpining for the trick
to move upswooping?
out of bounds your breath
fluid whispers, *here*

ON THE IDEAL FORM OF STUFFS

between release from the hand
and the hand that encloses, off the foot
lofting to what embrace, from the time
to lean in to the tug of lips
lies the stuff; the dream
does not teach enough
to see what is not material
how to commune sense
with cognition, or touch, or even
to absorb the lightning shock of her lips
her tongue her taste; instead we fall
in, to welcome the habited closing
of eyes and other sense, into
the folding eternal foundling
of this Her, in a woman for all
woman; yet the stuff of the spiral
the curving arc, the **poomf**
from the foot that makes heaven
the intent, the solid real of perfect
eternaling spiral, of tumbles
of parabola and the sounding pillow
on the lips of one's love

CONTRABAND

plums in the fridge
so sweet and so cool
carrot sticks and fruit
good for snacking
a tree in Eden:
these muffins are forbidden

THE MATH OF GIRL

infinity as symbol
the perseverings, the dogged
loving along the laborious trek
the she-eyes toward eternal faith
absconded with my daily disappointments
and faith re-inflated for this wretch
she counts me;
infinity as femi-logical
a woman as a series of eights
the hour-glass of shoulders
to hips vertically
the softer 8, and lateral
of breasts, and horizontal, hippish
heavens of gravity, and anchor
and this sickness unto health
to this fear, the trembling
toward the eternal

DUCK 129

once upon a time, there were atrocities
this is a poem of first love
a young girl of agnostic means
befriends a catholic boy
proud of his future, bound
by glories of a legended past
certain of nothing specific but
a fine GPA, some mathematical prowess
and a less gifted pen
she knowing much of escapes
into hope and future, much willing
to labor to feign what she
must, becomes who she would
would tire of second banana
but loved him immediately and hot
rolling him unwilling between heart and heat
dumped in a baptism of real awakenings
dumped agnostic in the middle of real love
sometimes safe, doubtlessly
knowing, young and alive
she tired, his unbelief waxing
her wherewithal receding, until finally
she believed him – love is Plato's curse
the body repulses the spirit, the mind
only soars so high as her breasts, her sex
her fire could suspend him

this is a song of reassurance
'I am better now' or 'no it never was
nor is now all about me' you taught
love without staying for exercises
of commencement, you are flown
because someone occasionally
learns on his own
a loving mentor and
in the best platonic tradition
you burn brightly in memory
and truth from afar

GAINING DUTZOW

here I bike my soft eyes
tearing to the wind tearing through my wet shirt
too cool too early of a morning in a Missouri May
having no secrets but this quiet trail
former railway through landscape
flowers, the river alongside to plot
my progress, slowed by the morning's northerlies
sun steaming my back, wind frosting my front
by rich woods and deep fields, I plod plodding
you, more deadly than heart's-bite descent
of memories, in moon-crystalled pools
padding toward me tipsy-toed
smiling a thousand years of love
under such trees of darkness
and full knowledge in what was
precocious and collapsing
we barely made that searing June
it may take years to mute
your floating joy to learn
my life, reward, compliance to this trail
I cycle centered between heat and cold
my eyes straining tears, westward
as today takes me to breakfast, biking
not without pain at heart and limbs keening
from my last hard dismount
have fallen torn, arisen trembling
will ride and will ride into this bite of wind

HARRY AND DAVID

we misread the card enclosed
failed to carry our date
of expiration; who knows
math any more or anyway
who truly cares? so today
seemed enough of an eternity
those lovely years of anniversaries
ago, from our foggy, furtive first
conversings to ticklish, wide-eyed
fearful fondlings were not
happy nothings but middle-life
cruxes, because at such junctures
if not crises, we find explication
for our moments' fateful fall
we lyricize, poeticize, pronounce
epiphanies grand, while we misread
the idiosyncratic scrawl
on the gift card that reminds
"this offer is limited"

HUSH

melt me
lip my eyes
nip my nose
forget what I
just mentioned
poetry by long distance
shades my darker moods
kiss me frightened
kiss me knowing
kiss me sacred
do not release
do not lose
this me
to words

BIRTHDAY

let psychologists opine
to the darkness
rush where angels fear
my life has been retort
response, contrapunto
I listened to every it seems
to them, their claims
have played every role I've read
and to which they willed me
have tried being all
they passing have wished
pretended a balance
of their hopes, my needs
needs? daily life daily
getting along on this curious
wondrous angelic
journey
with him
who can accept
I preferred peace
as I see this, our page
filling running out
who can know
who can judge

laying him down to sleep
I mix the pills as I am instructed
no one suggests, no one means
to urge my choice
this is our choice
take me my love as we
did so many abandoned
lost years ago
take me wholly
take me all
take me to sleep with you
and with this gun
I will close the door

MOTHER MALAWI

I have traced your alluvial in flood stage
planed your tectonic shelvings, have
fingered the dogstar scar of your upper
limb and smattered marveling
the peppered hues and topographic
freckling; kissed reverently your
scars of childbirth and gnawed
starving the spar of borrowed rib
feeding Mother, my goddess, my love

GODDESS MOM

Gaia our Mother knows heavens
reflected in our father's eyes
the wisdom of the firmament
prisms as vapors in Her hugging gaze
Her munificent orbs down-turned
deflect the horrors we need never learn
of want, from cold, the fear of cruelties
unmeted, among lessons keenly earned
and regales us from Her cosmos—of Ouranos
resolve and might; from Eros, how life musters
from the musted rage; to manifest in each smallest
guise Her cosmic, eternal and regenerating Love
from our Mother Goddess for each small wagging life
pupping happy in Her hugging grip

BETWEEN HEAVENS

a simple ontology really
all of us angelic messengers
with a limited number of years, and a mission
which only seems to vary
as the world on occasion seems
to wobble, our earthly placement
a mere figment of fixity

but each of us an angel with small gospels of love
and a life's moment in which to love
fully, truly, needly, properly
to sacrifice wholly for the need of one other
to bridge holiness down
to defer the earth-child from shame or sin
the clutch at loss, such varied sufferings
that skip each away from joy, the truths
daily of the smallest profoundest worlds

our birth is not a forgetting but the start
of a very brief race
to bestow the beauty of the enduring loveliness
of heaven
to share in each we find the awful certain
decisive knowing
that is eternal and to which each of us singularly returns
when like a switch our preset mission
is flipped

SKY

we seem to migrate
some do truly as we gape
at a flock wheeling into the morning air
we slowly, bi-pedally, motor
through days and loss to a place
higher than our former posts
so today you snag the key
to a new address, a keener
residence, a house that keens to home
all the while you wonder how
did I evolve to this now
who am I now or
why am I here *here*
where here is and who came with
birds I've heard align by
a metal chip in their brains ever
knowing north in contrast to south, west, east
you knowing now here, after the spasms
of hope, elation, hope, betrayal, hope, sadness
now here wondering upon what
promontory you now stand
while birds and some of us
naturally orient to know
where we've been all along

MARRY ME

I will never learn
another woman's body
as I know yours
I can never put
mine to work sufficient
as I labor at you

I will never learn
the cosmos as you
have set mine whirling
amid stars exploding
amid clouds of birth
I can never know
beyond the wisdom of you
the settled mythic gaze of you
as you create me over
and over again, can never
relearn the lessons of you
for how you school me
can never fathom
the deeps of you, can never
fulfill prerequisites for baccalaureate
of your conversely, universal love

I will never mine
the ore of anyone
will never sail the shores
of anywhere, will never
again touch the firmament
plunder paradise, monkey
the wrenches, bake the archetype
confabricate the wheeling
world since you

I should never try
the other poem
should abdicate the next
love letter, should rest
on the eighth day
except there is your mortal
immortal body schooling
me your moral syllabus
the library of our congress
the nightly all-nighters
postponing toward wisdom
you have given me up
to me, your dull boy, bound
again for commencement
seated raring first day
on your front row

FORD BABY

I'll give her another year
she's well worth the faith
though sentiment doesn't rev the engine
never had to, and I don't see why now
she's still as lovely as the first day
shiny, upright, factory-checked
with that smell you can't get
anywhere else but once

the years have not all been kind
but the good ones meld seamless
into memory, the taken
for granted guaranteed

she's high-built into the wind
shields against gales and strong storms
and years… another year I'll keep her
then half-years, then months
until we part at some point
mutually agreed on or some
preset (oh not by us) moment
of magic
or truth

ABOUT THE AUTHOR

John M. Yozzo is a native of Ponca City, OK, a graduate of the University of Tulsa, and Emeritus Professor of English from East Central University in Ada, OK. He lives in Tulsa.

CPSIA information can be obtained
at www.ICGtesting.com
Printed in the USA
LVHW032045230122
709126LV00005B/328